ECLIPSES

W9-ASK-652

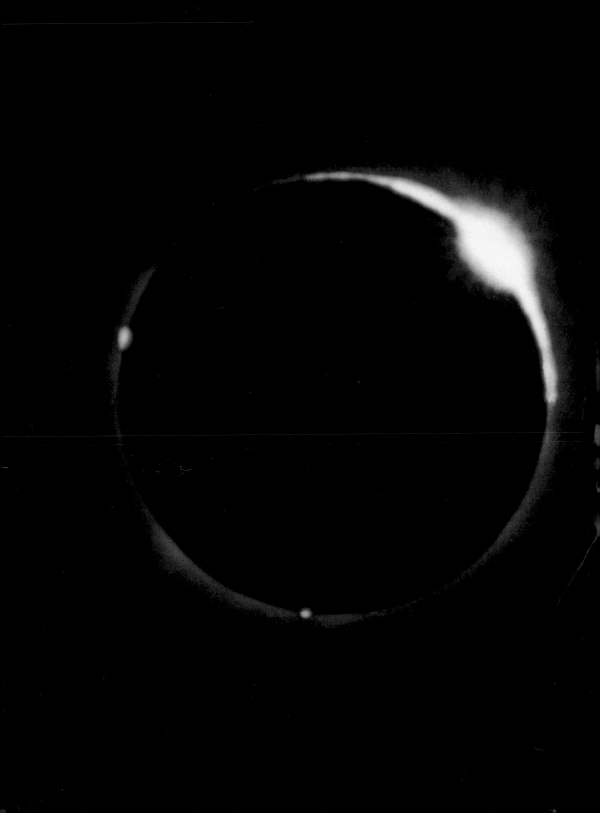

Nature's
Blackouts
ECLIPSES

by Billy Aronson

A First Book

FRANKLIN WATTS

A DIVISION OF GROLIER PUBLISHING
New York ■ London ■ Hong Kong ■ Sydney
Danbury, Connecticut

Cover photograph ©: Photo Researchers (David Leah/SPL)
Illustrations by MacArt Design

Photographs copyright ©: American Museum of Natural History: p. 37;
NASA: p. 2; NASA/JPL: p. 25; NOAO: p. 12; Peter Arnold, Inc.: p. 40
(Ray Pfortner); Photo Researchers: pp. 8, 33 (both photos by Rev. Ronald
Royer/SPL), 22, 38 (both photos by John Bova) 28, (George Post/SPL),
35 (Jerry Lodriguss), 48 (John Sanford/SPL), 50 (George East/SPL);
Reuters/Bettmann: pp. 46, 56; The Bettmann Archive: pp.10, 31.

Library of Congress Cataloging-in-Publication Data

Aronson, Billy
Eclipses: Nature's blackouts/ by Billy Aronson
p. cm. — (A First book)
Includes index.
Summary: Explains what causes eclipses of the sun and moon and describes
how they have been viewed and studied at different times in history.
ISBN 0-531-20238-0
1. Eclipses—Juvenile literature. [1. Eclipses.] I. Title. II. Series.
QB175.A76 1996
523.3'8—dc20   95-48847
                                                                  CIP AC

CONTENTS

ECLIPSES

As the moon reappears from an eclipse,
it looks eerily reddish.

ECLIPSE

Ancient China. One afternoon the sun suddenly vanishes, leaving towns and villages in total darkness. People tremble, scream, and weep, believing a dragon has swallowed up the sun.

Ancient Italy. Athenian warriors flee through the night after failing to capture Syracuse. They believe that they will be safe if they can just reach their ships and sail back to Greece. Just as they're about to board, they are astonished by what they see in the sky. First, the full moon is swept away by a dark shadow. When the moon returns, it is blood red. The Athenians think that what they have seen is a sign from the gods. They decide not to sail and are slaughtered by the enemy.

The weird, sudden disappearance of the moon could drive the ancients, like these Peruvians, into a frenzy.

Ancient Asia Minor (Turkey). As two armies wage gory battle, the sun begins to disappear. Moments later, it is almost completely gone. Suddenly, a brilliant halo flashes into view. Warriors on both sides are so awed by the heavenly spectacle that they forget about their anger and end their five-year war.

All over the ancient world, on every continent, from the dawn of recorded time, people have observed these remarkable events. Some people predicted them and were worshipped. Others failed to predict them and were executed.

Throughout history, these spectacles in the sky have caused people to faint, paint, prophesize, philosophize, weep, dance, worship, kill, tear their hair, hide their heads, fall to their knees, or simply stand and gaze. These bizarre happenings in the sky were impossible to ignore.

And they still are.

Modern Anyplace. Five teenagers drag themselves out of bed at three o'clock one autumn morning. They meet atop a mountain, stare at the full moon, and wait. One has brought along binoculars. Another has a camera and tripod. Suddenly, a curved shadow begins to creep across the moon.

After a few moments, the moon takes on a soft, rusty brown color.

Maybe Someday. You're walking home from school on a sunny, spring afternoon. Suddenly, you notice that the sky is growing darker, even though there are no rain clouds. You run inside your house, pull down your window shade, and pierce a small hole in the shade with a pin. Then you stare at the small circle of sunlight on the opposite wall. As the circle disappears, you realize that the sun has temporarily disappeared. You begin to understand the awe the ancients felt—and the fear.

How have the sun and moon managed to startle people again and again throughout history? The key to all these spectacular events and the unusual behavior they inspire can be described in one word: *eclipse*.

If you think the ancients were imagining things, this photograph will make you think again. The sun seems to have been swallowed up, leaving the day as dark as night.

ECLIPSE IN YOUR ROOM

If you look up eclipse in the dictionary, you will find that it means to hide something from view.

The word eclipse can be used to describe the way the glory of one achievement can overshadow the glory of another. For example, people feared that modern home run hitters Hank Aaron and Roger Marris would eclipse old home run champ Babe Ruth.

The word eclipse is most commonly used to describe what happens when the bright daytime sun or the glowing full moon is suddenly—but temporarily—shrouded in blackness.

If it's hard for you to imagine how one body in

the sky can hide another, think of ways *you* could position one body so that it would hide something else from your view. Look at the pictures below.

When the dog is in just the right position,
it blocks the girl's view of the lamp.

In the series of pictures on the previous page, the dog has moved its body between the lamp and the girl. When the dog positions itself just right, the brightness of the lamp is blocked from the girl's view.

In the series of pictures below, the girl has found a way to hide something else from her view: the dog. By standing in front of the lamp, she is able to completely cover the dog's body with her shadow, or *umbra*.

But her shadow doesn't always cover the dog completely. Before she reaches her final position, only part of the dog's body is covered by her shadow. This partial shadow is called a *penumbra*. The penumbra is the faint shadow that can be found on

As the girl moves between the lamp and the dog, her shadow covers more and more of the dog.

the edge of the umbra, or main shadow. As the girl moves closer to the dog, less of the shadow falling on the dog is penumbra and more is umbra.

This is how eclipses can occur right in your own room. These same basic types of eclipses happen in space. In space, however, the bodies eclipsing one another are not human bodies, or canine bodies, but *celestial* bodies—bodies in the sky.

Before you can understand eclipses of the sun and moon, you need to know a little bit about their relative positions in space. You also have to know about the ever-changing position of a third body— the one you live on.

AROUND AND AROUND AND AROUND

As you sit at your desk at school, it may be hard for you to imagine that Earth is moving. After all, your books aren't sliding across the desk. Your pencils aren't jiggling around. Your teacher isn't swaying back and forth. But Earth is moving—constantly. So are the other planets, the moon, the sun, and the entire *Milky Way galaxy*—the galaxy that includes our solar system.

How is Earth moving? For one thing, it's spinning. Our planet spins on its *axis*, the imaginary line through its center, spinning all the way around once a day.

Besides spinning on its axis, Earth revolves around the sun, completing an entire *revolution*

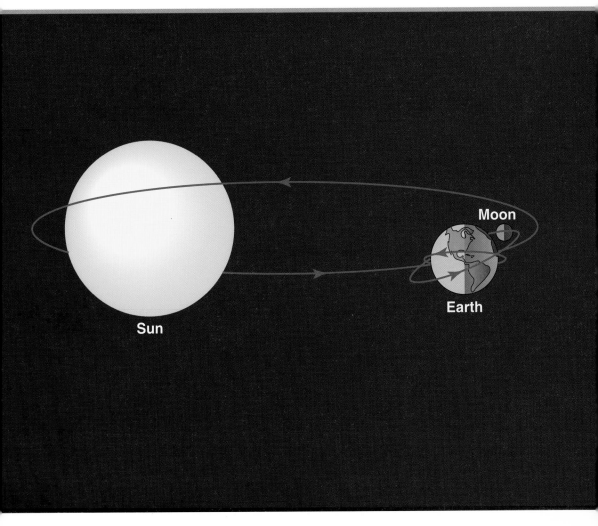

The moon revolves around Earth, which spins on its own axis while revolving around the sun.

once a year. Like a top that spins round and round while also moving across the floor, our planet moves in two ways at once.

While Earth is spinning around its axis and revolving around the sun, the moon is revolving around Earth. The moon goes around the Earth much more quickly than Earth goes around the sun. Although it takes Earth a year to go all the way around the sun, the moon completes a revolution in about a month.

As the diagram on the previous page shows, the *plane* in which the moon revolves around Earth is slightly different from the plane in which Earth revolves around the sun.

Think of the plane in which Earth revolves around the sun as a hula hoop floating on the water in a swimming pool. The moon's plane of rotation could be represented by a second hula hoop that is being held so that one side is partially above the water's surface and the other side is slightly below the water's surface. As the moon moves around and around the Earth, it goes above and below an imaginary line between the sun and Earth.

Although you don't feel Earth spinning or revolving, you witness the results of these movements every day and every night. When the side of Earth you live on spins away from the sun, the sky gets dark, and it becomes night. As your side of Earth spins around to face the sun, the sky becomes bright again, and it's morning.

You witness the results of the moon's movement too, every time you look into the sky on a clear night. Did you ever wonder why the moon seems to change shape? It's the same round moon up there every night. But as its position changes, so does its appearance to viewers on Earth.

Unlike the sun, the moon doesn't give off any light of its own. You only see the moon when it's lit up by that giant lamp in the sky: the sun.

The side of the moon that faces the sun is always bright, and the side that faces away is always dark. When the bright side of the moon faces the night side of Earth, you look up at the sky and see a bright, glowing full moon. As the moon moves around Earth, you see less and less of the bright side. About two weeks after you see a full moon, you see only a sliver of the moon. Then, one night, you can't see the moon at all.

When there's a "new moon," the bright side is turned completely away from Earth. Over the next couple of weeks, the moon appears to grow fuller and fuller each night. As the moon continues to revolve, more and more of its bright side is visible to viewers on Earth.

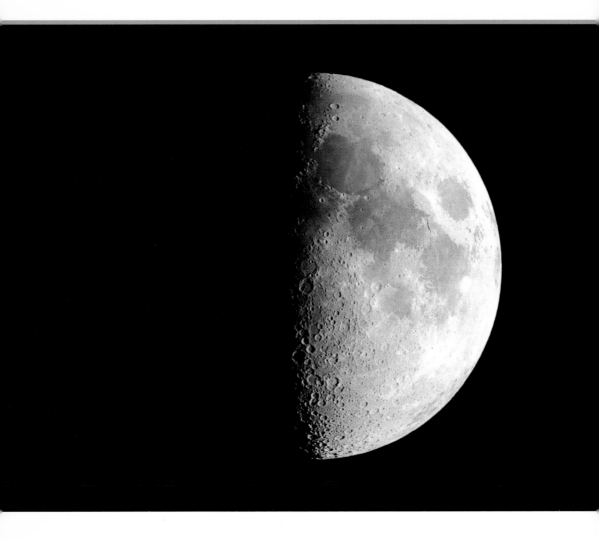

At different times the moon appears to take on various shapes, from a thin crescent to a full circle. This photograph shows how it appears on the eighth day of the lunar cycle.

If you stop to think about it, the changes caused by the movements of Earth and its moon are pretty extraordinary. The dazzling brightness of day is followed by swiftly falling darkness of night. There is a glowing shape in the night sky that is constantly changing. It swells from a sliver to a ball and then shrinks back again.

These things might not seem all that exciting to you. After all, they happen every day and every night. You just take them for granted.

But sometimes the sun, Earth, and moon can wind up in positions that force you to notice them. Can you imagine a position these three bodies could end up in that might cause ancient armies to lay down their weapons?

WHO TURNED OUT THE SUN?

CHAPTER 4

Have you ever found yourself suddenly in the dark? Maybe it happened during a power failure. Or when a light bulb burned out. Or when someone hit the light switch by mistake or tripped on an electric cord.

Even if you know the cause, finding yourself in the dark can be disorienting—and scary. Just imagine how scary it would be to find yourself in the dark because the sun has gone out! That's what it feels like during an eclipse of the sun, or *solar eclipse*.

During a solar eclipse, the moon blocks out the sun's light from viewers on Earth, just as the dog in Chapter 2 blocked out the light of the lamp from the girl's view.

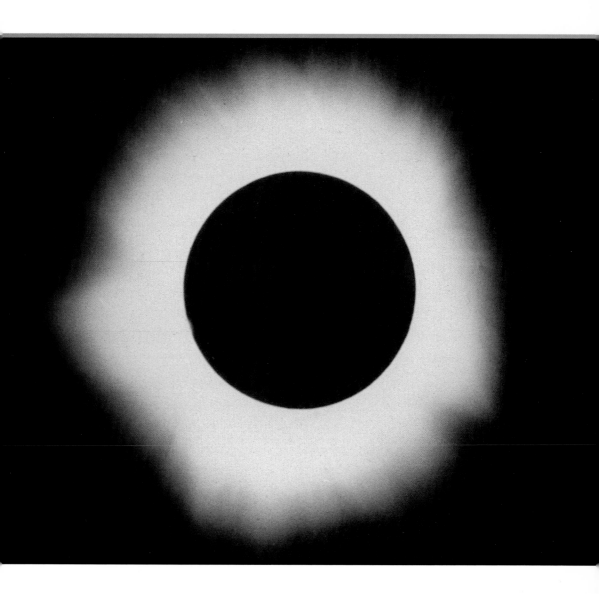

During a solar eclipse, the moon blocks out the sun's light from viewers on Earth.

It wasn't hard for the dog to block the light from the lamp because the dog was larger than the lamp. The moon, however, is thousands of times smaller than the sun. So for the moon to block the sun's light from viewers on Earth, all three bodies must be very precisely placed.

The moon passes between the sun and Earth at some point during each revolution. Most of the time, the moon is slightly above or below the plane of the sun and Earth when it passes between them. For the moon to block the sun from viewers on Earth, it must pass between those bodies just as it's rising or falling into their plane. A solar eclipse can only take place if the sun, moon, and Earth lie in a perfectly straight line.

But even if all three bodies are perfectly aligned, an eclipse may not occur. The distance between Earth and the moon must also be just right. When this distance is just right, the sun and the moon appear to be exactly the same size when viewed from Earth.

As the diagram indicates, when the three bodies line up in a pefectly straight line, the dark side of the moon is facing Earth. The diagram also shows why a solar eclipse takes place during the daytime. You can only see the sun being blocked when you're on the side of the Earth facing the sun—the day side.

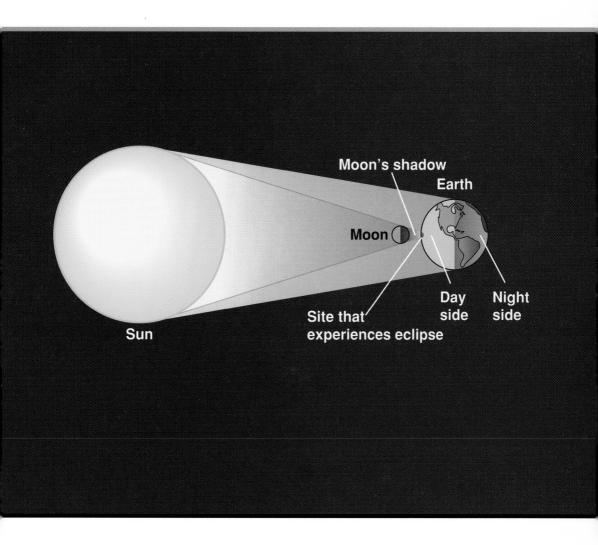

During a solar eclipse, Earth moves between the sun and the moon. Observers on the night side of the Earth lose sight of the moon for a few hours.

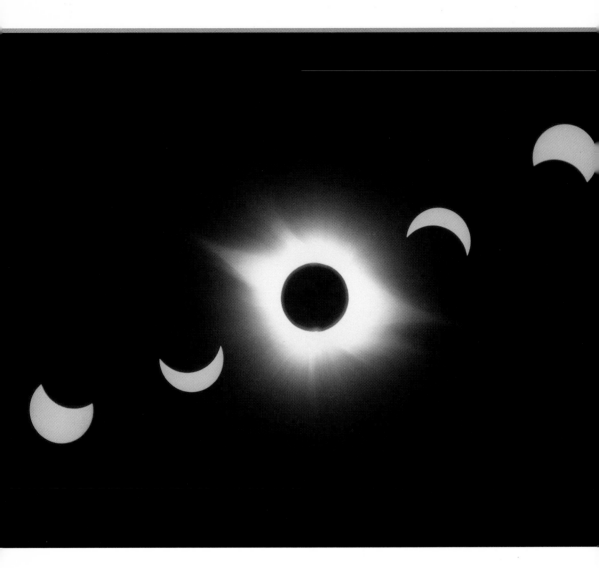

As the moon moves in front of the sun, the sun appears in the shape of a crescent that quickly shrinks away, and then reappears.

Total Eclipse

The most impressive type of solar eclipse is called a *total eclipse*. During a total solar eclipse, the sun is totally blocked by the moon. As a total solar eclipse begins, the sky darkens. The temperature falls a few degrees because the amount of light and heat reaching a small part of the Earth decreases.

Humans aren't the only ones that notice these sudden changes. Cows, dogs, and ants suddenly may stop whatever they're doing. Birds stop chirping. Flower petals close. No wonder solar eclipses made ancient humans think all life might be coming to an end!

Soon the sun appears in a shape that you usually associate with the moon—a crescent. But this crescent shrinks a lot faster than the crescent moon does. As it shrinks, darkness sweeps across Earth.

Sometimes, as the crescent becomes very thin, stripes of darkness called *shadow bands* rush across the ground. Shadow bands are caused by the *atmosphere*, the many-layered blanket of gases that surrounds Earth.

Different layers of the atmosphere have different temperatures. As rays of sunlight move from one layer to the next, they shift position. Because there are fewer rays of sunlight during an eclipse, you can see the effect of their shifting in the bands of shadow that ripple across Earth.

If the wavy motion of shadow bands reminds you of the waves that appear in the air above a hot barbecue, it's no coincidence. Both phenomena are caused by light passing through gases of different temperatures.

When the moon is about to cover the sun, the last sliver of sunlight provides viewers with a glimpse of spectacular solar jewels called *Baily's beads*. Baily's beads, named after Francis Baily who wrote about the phenomenon in 1836, are huge spheres of glowing light. They form when rays from the sun are scattered by valleys and mountains on the edge of the moon.

Sometimes this phenomenon creates the image of a single breathtaking jewel. When the rays shine through a deep lunar valley, they form a dazzling spark. This burst of light is smaller than other Baily's beads, but more intense. Appearing in the sliver of crescent sun, this spark looks like a precious diamond in a glowing diamond ring.

And then it happens—the sun is completely covered. People who observe a total eclipse are struck by the perfect fit between the moon and the sun. They seem to be just the same shape, just the right size, and just the right distance apart. It

As the sun's rays are scattered by the edge of the moon, they can form a burst of light that looks like a diamond ring.

seems almost as though the moon was specially designed to cover the sun, like a lens cap made to snap right into place over a camera's lens.

The period during which the moon hides the sun is called *totality*. Throughout totality daylight is blocked out, and a region of Earth is plunged into darkness. But what's really surprising about this darkness is how many things it allows you to see.

Do you like to listen to loud music at night? When you turn your music off, are you ever struck by how many different sounds you suddenly hear? Maybe you hear music being played downstairs or next door. You might also hear the hum of a dishwasher, muffled laughter outside, creaking tree branches, chirping crickets, screeching tires, or sirens screaming in the distance. All of these sounds were being made before, but they were completely drowned out by the music blaring in your room.

Just as blaring music drowns out other sounds, the blazing rays of sunlight that normally fill the sky make it impossible for you to see many other things. During a solar eclipse, when these rays are blocked out, viewers on Earth can behold rare heavenly sights.

The layer of the sun from which sunlight comes is called the *photosphere*. During an eclipse, rays

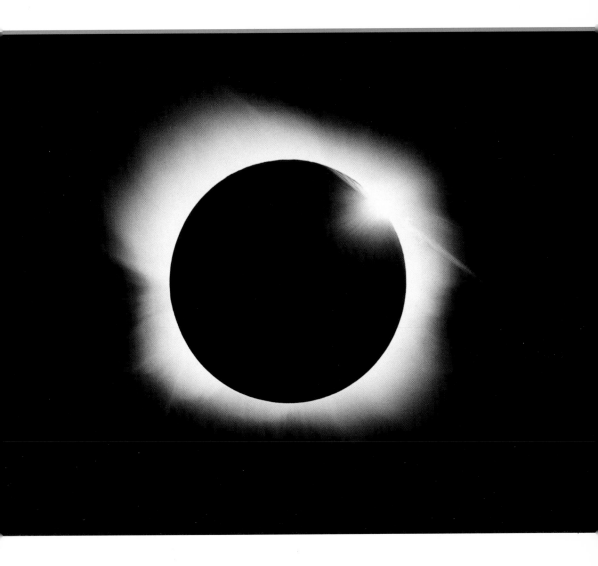

During a solar eclipse, rays from the sun's photosphere are blocked out. The light we see comes from the chromosophere.

from the photosphere are blocked out, so rays coming from the sun's other layers become visible.

As totality begins, a rosy glow appears behind the moon. This glow comes from the *chromosphere*, the layer that lies just beneath the photosphere.

But the layer of the sun that is most striking during a solar eclipse is its outermost layer—the *corona*. Throughout totality the corona's pearly soft light can be seen. It reaches way out beyond the black moon, like petals on a giant flower.

Even more striking are the bright red plumes that shoot out from behind the moon. *Prominences*, as they are called, look like frozen flames. But they're really streams of glowing gas that leap from the sun and extend hundreds of thousands of miles into space.

Besides those solar sights, the brightest stars and planets become visible. These bodies appear in the daytime sky, but are usually washed out by sunlight.

All good things must come to an end. As the moon continues moving across the sun, totality ends. Baily's beads or the diamond ring may reappear on the opposite side of the moon. Then a sliver of sun peeks out and increases in size until daylight is restored.

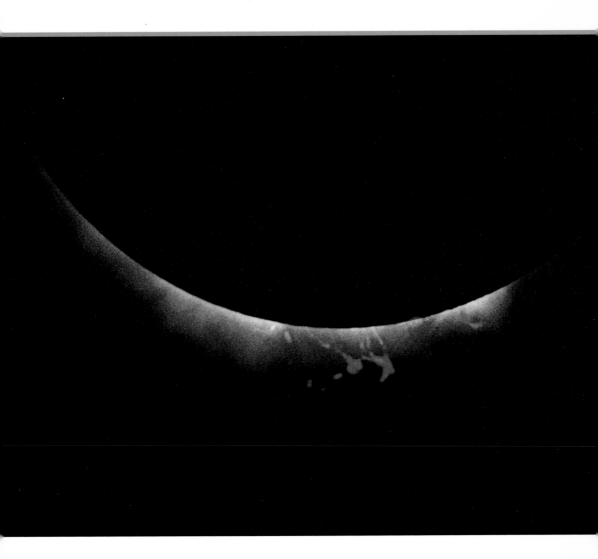

When the sun's bright rays are blocked by the moon, red plumes of light called prominences can be seen reaching out from the sun's surface.

Beasts frolic, ants crawl, birds chirp, and people continue their daily activities. But what spectacular sights they've witnessed—and all within a matter of minutes. Totality never lasts longer than seven minutes, and it's usually much shorter.

Partial Eclipse

Of course, if the solar eclipse isn't a total eclipse, there's no totality at all. When Earth, moon, and sun don't quite line up, the result is a *partial eclipse*. During a partial eclipse only part of the moon covers the sun, so the sun remains visible. Viewers might notice that it's a little darker. But the effect isn't much different than when the sky suddenly becomes cloudy.

Even when the three bodies fall into a straight line, there won't be a total eclipse if the moon is too far from Earth. Why does the moon's distance from Earth change? Because its *orbit* isn't round—it's egg-shaped, or elliptical. To block all of the sun's rays from Earth, the moon must be in the part of its orbit that comes closest to Earth.

Annular Eclipse

During most of its orbit the moon is too far away from Earth for a total solar eclipse to occur. If the moon is in a part of its orbit that is far away from Earth when

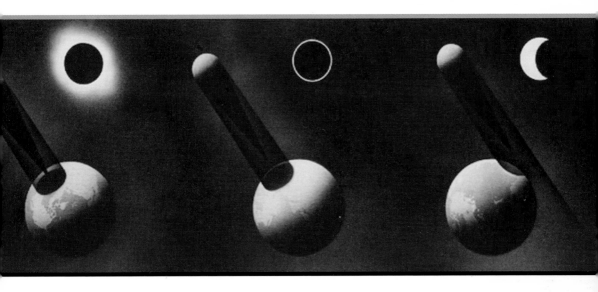

The images above show how the moon and Earth are positioned during a total eclipse, an annular eclipse, and a partial eclipse.

it passes between Earth and the sun, the result is called an *annular eclipse*. Like a partial solar eclipse, an annular eclipse isn't nearly as exciting as a total eclipse.

Although the moon passes right in front of the sun, it's too far away to block it out. The moon appears to be much smaller than the disk of sun. A ring of sunlight remains visible, and the sun's corona, chromosphere, and prominences cannot be seen.

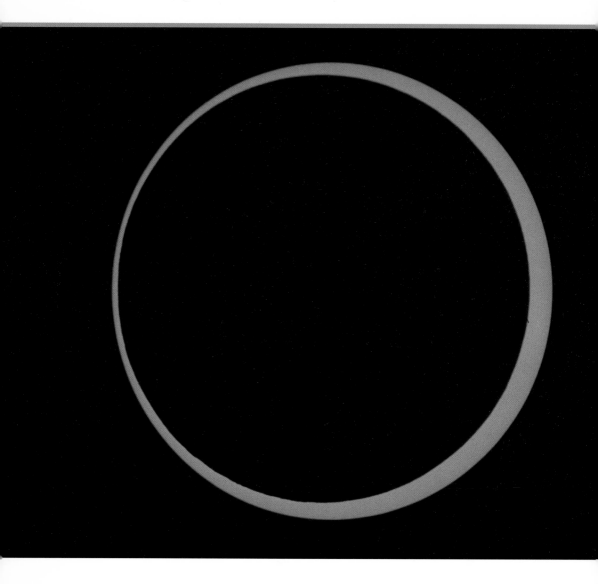

During an annular eclipse, a ring of sunlight remains visible around the moon.

Viewing a Total Solar Eclipse

When a total eclipse does occur, you've got to be in just the right place at the right time or you'll miss it. The section of Earth from which a total solar eclipse can be viewed is called the *path of totality*. Because the moon is so small compared to the sun, the path of totality is usually far less than 100 miles (160 km) wide. So a total solar eclipse might be visible in one town, while people in a neighboring town see only a partial eclipse.

Could you wait for totality to come to you? You could. But it might be a long wait! A total solar eclipse is only visible from any given spot on Earth every 360 years.

Many people don't wait for solar eclipses to come to them. They go to eclipses. Die-hard eclipse lovers find out when and where eclipses are going to occur from astronomy books or journals. Then they travel far and wide to experience the thrill of totality.

But there's another catch for people trying to see a total solar eclipse. That's right, yet another catch. Besides the fact that the three heavenly bodies have to line up completely. And that they have to be just the right distances apart. And that you have to be within the narrow path of totality.

By using binoculars to focus the sun's light on the ground, this man creates a circle of sunlight, which shrinks as the eclipse approaches totality. At this point it's about halfway there, as you can see from the yellow half-circle on the rock.

And that totality only lasts a few minutes, at most. The last, most frustrating catch is that even when you're in just the right position to view a solar eclipse, you can't look up at it!

You'd never think of staring up at the sun on a sunny day. Even glancing near that burning ball makes you squint and look away.

When the sun's light is blocked out, it's easy to look up at the sun. You don't feel any urge to look away—but you should. Even when nearly all sunlight is blocked out, its radiation pours down past the moon. Staring up at the eclipsed sun can be just as harmful to your eyes as staring at the sun any other time. It can cause permanant eye damage, even blindness.

Scientists have special instruments that allow them to look at the sun as totality approaches. But you don't need a special instrument. You can keep track of what the sun is doing by simply staring at the ground.

Stand beneath a tree, stare at the ground, and watch what happens to a beam of light that has passed through the spaces between the leaves above your head. As the sun becomes a shrinking crescent, so will the circle of light at your feet.

There's even a way to observe the eclipse from inside your school or house. Cut a hole in a piece of cardboard, allow sunlight to pass through the hole, and watch what happens when the light hits the wall of your room.

A solar eclipse is hard to find, dangerous to observe, and over much too quickly. But, luckily, there's another kind of eclipse. It is visible over huge areas of the planet. You can stare right up at it without any danger. And it can last for hours!

But this second kind of eclipse doesn't take place during the day, like a solar eclipse. It only happens at night.

WHO TURNED OUT THE MOON?

CHAPTER 5

C hapter 4 described how one body can make another appear dark by blocking out its light source. But there's another way one body can eclipse another.

Remember the girl in Chapter 2? First, she hid the lamp from view by having her dog sit in front of it. Then she made the dog appear dark by covering it with her shadow.

Viewers on Earth can see the moon darkened by a shadow. The diagram on the next page shows how this can—and does—happen. The result is called an eclipse of the moon, or *lunar eclipse*.

During a lunar eclipse, the sun, Earth, and the moon are in a straight line, as in a solar eclipse. Except this time, the moon isn't in the middle— Earth is. As a result, Earth casts a shadow on the

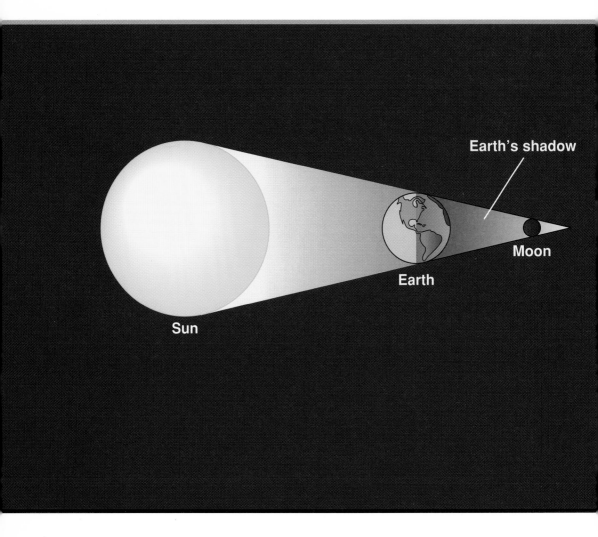

During a lunar eclipse, the sun, Earth, and moon line up in such a way that the moon appears dark to viewers on one side of Earth.

moon. This darkening is visible from the side of Earth facing the moon—the night side. This is why you can only witness a lunar eclipse at night.

Another thing you can count on during a lunar eclipse is that it will only occur when there's a full moon. That's because when the sun, Earth, and the moon line up, the moon's bright side is facing Earth's dark side. As the eclipse begins, that full moon starts looking less and less full.

Earth's penumbra reaches the moon about 30 minutes before the umbra does. So, at first, the moon just appears a little dimmer. But when the umbra hits, you can see a dark curve slip across the moon.

Have you ever walked in front of a film projector and noticed the shadow of the top of your head on the screen? That's similar to what happens as a lunar eclipse begins. But instead of viewing a shadow of your head, you're viewing a shadow of your planet!

The moon doesn't always stay dark during a lunar eclipse. The instant it becomes dark, something surprising may happen—it may turn red, orange, or even brown. The dog didn't turn red when the girl covered him with her shadow. A movie screen wouldn't turn orange if you covered it with your shadow. So why does the moon?

This photograph shows the moon at various points during a lunar eclipse. As Earth's umbra moves across the moon, the moon seems to be shrinking away.

That Red Light

To understand the reddish light covering the moon, you have to understand the reddish light that's pouring in through your window right now. And zooming down from the ceiling. And bouncing off the letters on this page. This reddish light passes by you all the time, but you rarely see it. That's because the red light is only one part of the white light that surrounds you.

The white light from your lamps and from the sun is made up of red, orange, yellow, green, blue, and violet rays of light. You can see these individual colors—as a rainbow—when sunlight is broken up by water particles in the air. All the colors of a rainbow are mixed together in the light you see all the time.

Light travels through space in waves. Each color of light has its own shape. Waves of blue and violet light are shorter than waves of red and orange light.

As rays of sunlight pass by the edges of Earth, they travel through Earth's atmosphere. Although the rays move through empty space without any trouble, they begin to collide with lots of particles when they hit Earth's atmosphere. The atmosphere is an obstacle course for light rays!

The longer waves have an easier time passing through the atmosphere. So a few reddish rays

During a lunar eclipse, sunlight passes through Earth's atmosphere on its way to the moon. Of all the colors mixed together in sunlight, the rays of red light pass through the atmosphere most easily. So the moon takes on a reddish glow.

often slip around Earth, casting a faint red, orange, or brown glow on the darkened moon. (Gorgeous rosy sunsets are also caused by sunlight that has been broken up by the atmosphere.)

Viewing Lunar Eclipses

As with solar eclipses, lunar eclipses aren't always total. There are two other kinds of lunar eclipses that may occur if the moon, sun, and Earth don't line up just right. In one type, a *penumbral lunar eclipse*, the moon only passes through Earth's penumbra. In this case, the moon is only faintly dimmed. In the other case, a *partial lunar eclipse*, Earth's shadow passes over part of the moon, but never darkens it completely.

There are only about two or three lunar eclipses each year, as opposed to about four or five solar eclipses. But in any given year, you're far more likely to see a lunar eclipse than a solar eclipse. A solar eclipse is only visible across a narrow band of ground, but a lunar eclipse is visible across the entire dark side of the planet.

Anyone who can see the moon can see the eclipse! While a total solar eclipse can't be viewed by people in San Francisco and Los Angeles at the same time, a total lunar eclipse can be watched simultaneously by people in Alaska and Brazil.

During a partial lunar eclipse, only part of the moon darkens. Note the reddish glow, though it's far less apparent here than in the photograph of a total lunar eclipse.

Another reason that lunar eclipses are easier to see than solar eclipses is because they last much longer—up to 4 hours.

And you don't have to spend those hours staring at the ground or at a wall. You can stare straight up at the moon because it is lit by reflected sunlight, not direct sunlight. There is no need to worry about excess radiation. So you won't harm your eyes by staring at it, any more than you would get a moonburn by lying out beneath it.

Slow, mysterious lunar eclipses can give you thrills. And quick, dazzling solar eclipses can give you thrills. But eclipses give scientists more than thrills. They give them precious clues.

DARK SPHERES, BRIGHT IDEAS

CHAPTER 6

Has anything like this ever happened to you?

You accidentally knock a clock to the floor. Although the clock is still ticking, it's cracked wide open. You're angry. You're upset.

But you're also delighted. For years you've watched those hands go around, listened to the ticking, and heard the buzzing of the alarm. Now, for once, you can peer into the intricate machinery that's been making all those things happen. You feel lucky. You finally have a chance to peek inside this machine that's been a big part of your life.

Similarly, eclipses give scientists a special chance to peek into a machine that fascinates them: the universe. By studying the times eclipses occur and the places from which they're visible, scientists were able to figure out the exact positions of the sun, moon, and Earth relative to one another.

By studying the way the surface of the moon responds to darkness during a lunar eclipse, scientists learned about its chalky texture and about the amount of dust in Earth's atmosphere. By studying the area around the sun during a solar eclipse, scientists discovered new comets. By studying the light of the sun's corona during solar eclipses, scientists learned about the surface of the sun.

By studying the way a solar eclipse works, scientists figured out how to build a *coronagraph*—an instrument that blocks out light from the photosphere as the moon does during a solar eclipse. Using the coronagraph, scientists can study the sun's chromosphere all year long.

One of the most exciting tests done during an eclipse verified Albert Einstein's *theory of relativity*. According to Einstein, the pull of gravity exerted by a huge object is so strong that it can pull beams of light and change their direction. For example, Einstein said the sun's gravity could pull rays of light coming from distant stars in toward the sun as they passed by. But how could anyone hope to test this? To study beams of light passing by the sun, you'd need to see them. And you can't see much near the sun besides the sun's own bright rays—except during a solar eclipse.

So during a total solar eclipse, scientists took pictures of the light coming from distant stars in the part of the sky close to the sun's position. The photographs revealed that the rays had indeed been pulled in toward the sun. Thanks to the solar eclipse, scientists could prove that the theory was right.

A COSMIC COINCIDENCE

Unlike ancient humans, we know a lot about eclipses. We know what causes them. We know when and where to expect them. We know how to view them safely. We even know how to learn more about the universe by studying them with complex instruments. We sure have come a long way since ancient times!

But knowing about eclipses doesn't make them any less interesting. In fact, the more you know, the more interesting they seem.

Think about how many coincidences it takes to make eclipses possible. If the Earth didn't have a moon, no one on Earth would ever see an eclipse. But just having a moon isn't enough. The moon's,

Earth's, and sun's sizes, shapes, distances apart, and orbits all had to be just right—or there'd be no eclipses, ever.

Eclipses are cosmic coincidences. When you consider how much coincidence is involved, eclipses seem almost as miraculous as rainbows, lightning, or the starry sky itself. You know much more than the ancients did about eclipses. But when you see one, you can still be startled. You can still be thrilled. And you can still be amazed at the wondrous workings of the universe.

Although we now know what causes them, eclipses continue to impress, entertain, and mystify.

GLOSSARY

annular eclipse—an eclipse in which the sun is not completely blocked by the moon.

atmosphere—the layer of air and other gases that separates Earth from space.

axis—the imaginary line through the center of Earth or other celestial body about which that body rotates.

Baily's beads—huge spheres of glowing light that can be seen just before a total solar eclipse.

celestial—of, or relating to, the sky or the heavens.

chromosphere—a layer of the sun. Light emitted from the chromosphere is only visible during a total solar eclipse.

corona—the outermost layer of the sun.

coronagraph—an instrument that blocks out light from the photosphere, as the moon does during a total solar eclipse. Scientists can use it to study light from the chromosphere at any time.

eclipse—a phenomenon that occurs when an object is blocked by something else.

lunar eclipse—when the moon is hidden by a shadow cast by Earth as it moves between the sun and the moon.

Milky Way galaxy—the name of the galaxy that we live in.

orbit—to circle another body. The moon orbits Earth, and Earth orbits the sun.

partial eclipse—an eclipse in which the sun is partially blocked out by the moon.

partial lunar eclipse—an eclipse in which the Earth's shadow passes over part of the moon.

path of totality—the section of Earth from which a solar eclipse can be viewed.

penumbra—a partial shadow cast over an object.

penumbral lunar eclipse—a lunar eclipse in which the moon passes through Earth's penumbra. As a result, the moon remains visible, but shines less brightly.

photosphere—the layer of the sun from which sunlight comes.

plane—a flat or level surface.

prominences—bright red plumes that shoot out from behind the moon during a total solar eclipse.

revolution—one trip around the sun.

shadow bands—stripes of darkness that rush across the ground just before a total solar eclipse.

solar eclipse—when the moon moves between Earth and the sun.

theory of relativity—one of Albert Einstein's theories. It states that the pull of gravity exerted by a huge object is so strong that it can change the direction in which a beam of light is traveling.

total eclipse—an eclipse in which the sun is completely blocked out by the moon.

totality—the part of a solar eclipse in which the moon prevents all of the sun's light from reaching Earth.

umbra—a conical shadow cast over an object.

FOR FURTHER READING

Calvin, William H. *How the Shaman Stole the Moon*. New York: Bantam, 1991.

Schaaf, Fred. *Wonders of the Sky: Observing Rainbows, Comets, Eclipses, the Stars and Other Phenomena*. Mineola, NY: Dover Publications, 1983.

INTERNET RESOURCES

Steve Albers' Astro Images and Photographs
http://www.fsl.noaa.gov/frdbin/albers.astphotos.cgi

Astronomy
http://www.kalmbach.com/astro/astronomy.html

INDEX

Page numbers in *italics* indicate illustrations.

ABOUT THE AUTHOR

Billy Aronson's other science books include two published by W. H. Freeman: *They Came from DNA*, which was named a NSTA/CBC Outstanding Science Book for Children in 1994, and *Scientific Goofs*, which has been printed in English, Chinese, and Turkish.

Billy's television writing credits include PBS's *Reading Rainbow* and *Where in Time Is Carmen Sandiego?*, CBS's *Really Wild Animals*, The History Channel's *Year by Year for Kids*, and MTV's *Beavis and Butt-Head,* as well as shows for Comedy Central, HBO, Nickelodeon, the Cartoon Network, and Children's Television Workshop. He is also a playwright, with a play featured in *Best American Short Plays 1992–93* (Applause Books).

Billy lives in Brooklyn with his wife, Lisa Vogel, and their children, Jake and Anna.